Stock Market Trivia

Including a Special Section:

The Weird Words of Wall Street

Fred Fuld III

No part of this book may be reproduced, stored in a retrieval system, or transmitted by any means in whole or in part without the express written permission of the author.

All trademarks, registered trademarks, service marks, and registered service marks are owned by their respective trademark, registered trademark, service mark, and registered service mark owners. Images of certificates are shown for educational purposes.

This publication is sold with the understanding that the author and publisher are not engaged in providing investment advice, tax advice or legal advice. No recommendations, either expressed or implied, are being made to buy, sell, hold or short any of the mentioned stocks. No legal, tax or accounting advice is expressed or implied. The advice of a professional should be consulted if investment expertise is required. The author and publisher specifically disclaim any liability that is incurred from the use of the content of this book. Information provided in the book is believed to be accurate but is not guaranteed. From time to time, the author may own stocks mentioned in this book.

CONTENTS

Fred Fuld III

INTRODUCTION

If you are interested in learning how to invest or what stocks to buy, you are looking at the wrong book. This book won't give you any investment advice, nor will it give you any stock trading tips.

The purpose of this book is to provide interesting, amusing, and fascinating trivia about Wall Street and the stock market. Did a stock really trade for over a million dollars a share? What stock had the symbol GRRR and why? Can the company's stock symbol affect the stock's price? What company paid $8.5 million for a domain name? What stock owned George Washington's graffiti on a rock?

If you want to know the answers to these investment and stock market questions, and many, many others, you have come to the right place. I mention numerous stocks in this book. Because I include them does not mean that they are good stocks or bad stocks. It just means there is something either interesting or out of the ordinary about the company that I thought readers would like to hear about.

Some people think that finance is boring. This book will put an end to that misconception. Enjoy the trivia.

Chapter 1
No Bull about Bulls and Bears

A bull is someone who believes the stock market will go up and a bear is someone who believes the stock market will go down. A bull market is a rising market and a bear market is a falling market.

Where does bull and bear come from? Some sources say that a bull knocks you up in the air (rising market) and a bear knocks you down (falling market). However, there were some old proverbs floating around Europe during the 1700's. In Germany, the saying was 'Don't sell the bear-skin before you have killed the bear.' In Holland, they said 'Don't sell the bearskin before the bear is dead.' In Italy, they said 'Don't sell the bearskin before you have caught the bear.' In England, the saying was 'Don't sell the bearskin before the bear is caught.' In all cases, they said the same thing, 'Don't sell something you don't have.'

The book, *Every Man His Own Broker*, published in 1775, contains the first usage of the words Bull and Bear as types of investors. It was written by Thomas Mortimer, and published by S. Hooper in London. The words Bulls and Bears are mentioned several times throughout the book, including the Preface. This book has some great quotes. In the Preface he talks about the "Act for the better preventing the infamous practice of Stock-jobbing; by which the most palpable and glaring frauds then in vogue, were indeed suppressed: the Bubbles burst, and the Racehorses of

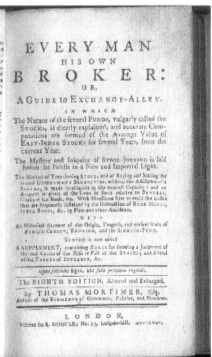

Exchange Alley, expired with the date of that act; but BULLS and BEARS still exist in full vigour."

In addition to Bulls and Bears, he also mentions on page 69 another animal, "lame duck." He describes lame ducks as "those who refuse to fulfill their contracts." This related to what short sellers did (and still do). A short seller is someone who does a stock transaction in the hopes that a stock will drop in price. A short sale is when an investor sells a stock that he doesn't have (he technically borrows the stock from the brokerage firm to sell) then buys it back at a later time at, hopefully, a lower price (when he technically takes the stock that he bought and returns it to the brokerage firm). The difference between the sale price and purchase price is his profit (or loss if he has to buy it back at a higher price).

Short selling also led to another old saying "He who sells what isn't his'n, must buy it back or go to prison."

Anyway, that covers the bears, how about the bulls? Just like donkeys and elephants, there had to be an alternative animal. The bull seemed a natural contrast, an animal that charges ahead, moves forward, and is strong and powerful (just like a strong stock market).

As long as we are covering old sayings, make sure you stay away from the stock brokerage firms who's motto is "Win 'em, spin 'em, churn 'em, and burn 'em." That means win the client over, give them a good spin story about a stock, get them to do as many trades as possible whether it's good for them or not (which is known in the industry as churning), and keep doing it until you have used up all their money.

PREFACE. xv

his long and faithful fervices in parliament, fome regulations propofed by him, were paffed into a law, in the year 1734, under the title of " *An act for the better preventing the infamous practice of Stock-jobbing*;" by which the moft palpable and glaring frauds then in vogue, were indeed fuppreffed : the BUBBLES burft, and the RACE HORSES of Exchange-Alley, expired with the date of that act; but BULLS and BEARS ftill exift in full vigour. The rejected part of Sir John Barnard's fcheme for the total extirpation of Stock-jobbers, was brought into parliament laft feffions with fome alterations, and was again thrown out by the houfe of lords; and fuch muft be the fate of all fchemes of the fame nature, in which public regifters are propofed to be kept, of thofe

6.

Chapter 2

Pink Sheet Stocks: Why are they Pink and are there any Other Sheet Colors?

Many times you will hear that a stock is traded on the "Pink Sheets". What does that mean, why do they call them pink sheet stocks, and where did the name come from?

Pink Sheet stocks are over-the-counter stocks that are not traded as often as NASDAQ stocks or Over-the-Counter Bulletin Board stocks. This could be due to the fact that they are penny stocks, in bankruptcy, or closely held public companies for which not many shares are available for public trading. There are currently over 20,000 of these companies. They are sometimes designated with a .pk at the end of the stock symbol. These stocks are bought from Market Makers, which are brokerage firms that agree to buy the stocks and sell the stocks at specific prices generally at all times.

Currently, the list of market makers is provided electronically, but originally they were listed on long pieces of pink paper stapled at the top, and were provided to stock brokerage firms on a daily basis, which listed the name of the stock, the market maker, and the bid and asked prices. These  were printed by the National Quotation Bureau since 1913. The company also published Yellow Sheets which listed over-the-counter corporate bonds. In 2000, the company changed its name to Pink Sheets LLC, and eight years later to Pink OTC Markets, and finally to OTC Markets Group.

Back in the 1970's and 1980's, another company printed a listing of municipal bond offerings that were available for purchase in the after-market by brokerage firms and investors. It was in a booklet form printed on blue paper. These booklets were colloquially referred to as Blue Sheets.

Chapter 3

The Stock that Owned a Rock with George Washington's Graffiti

Natural Bridge of Virginia Inc. is one of the publicly traded companies that owned an unusual item, the arched limestone boulder, 50 feet wide at its narrowest, which supports Route 11 over Cedar Creek in Virginia. This 100 Million year old bridge, 215 feet tall and 90 feet across, was considered one of the Seven Natural Wonders of the World during the 1800's, more popular than Niagara Falls. When George Washington, the famous first president of the United States, was a young man, he worked as a surveyor for Lord Fairfax. During the 1750's, he surveyed the area where the natural bridge exists, and committed the unconscionable act (worse than chopping down a cherry tree) of writing graffiti, carving his initials on the bridge's wall.

The also famous third president of the United States, Thomas Jefferson, bought the Natural Bridge and the surrounding 150 odd acres for the grand total of only 20 shilling several years later, in July of 1774; not as good a price as the island of Manhattan but still a good deal. He took it off the hands of King George III of England.

The site remained in the hands of the Jefferson family until 1833, and used as a retreat for their family and guests. At that time, it was purchased by a private organization which built a hotel to house the large number of visitors to the site. The guests had the option of being lowered over the edge in a steel cage in order to get a better view of the underside of the bridge. A violinist would play background music during the drop.

During the later half of the twentieth century, the company that owned the bridge was publicly traded. The company's source of income came from the sales from the gift shop. They had 163,700 shares outstanding, paid their last dividend of 15 cents a share on November 30, 1985. On April 4, 1988, the company was acquired by

Bridge Associates, Inc. at a price of $42 per common share. The shares that were not tendered for the cash purchase price continued to trade very sporadically. It was last quoted at a bid price of $14 per share on September 28, 1990.

Chapter 4

Original Dow Jones Industrial Average Stocks: Where Are They Now?

"The man who begins to speculate in stocks with the intention of making a fortune usually goes broke, whereas the man who trades with a view of getting good interest on his money sometimes gets rich."

~ *Charles Dow, 1901*

The original twelve Dow Jones Industrial Average stocks was a list that was developed by Charles Dow on May 26, 1896, for his small publication called the *Customer's Afternoon Letter*. This letter eventually became *The Wall Street Journal*. The following is the original list of stocks and what eventually happened to them.

- American Cotton Oil - became a company that was eventually taken over by Unilever
- American Sugar - now known as Domino Foods, Inc.
- American Tobacco - due to an antitrust ruling, it was split apart in the early 1900's
- Chicago Gas - taken over by People's Gas in the late nineteenth century, which was later taken over by Integrys Energy Group.
- Distilling and Cattle Feeding - eventually became part of Millennium Chemicals
- General Electric - still General Electric
- Laclede Gas - still the same company but known as the Laclede Group

9

- National Lead - now known as NL Industries
- North American - In 1946, the Securities & Exchange Commission forced the company to break apart
- Tennessee Coal, Iron and Railroad - taken over by U. S. Steel in 1907
- U.S. Leather preferred - went out of business in 1952
- U.S. Rubber - became Uniroyal, taken over by B. F. Goodrich, which was taken over by Michelin

Charles Dow was born November 6, 1851 on a Sterling, Connecticut farm. Since his father died when he was only six years old, he worked odd jobs as a child and never even finished high school. He began his career as a reporter for a Massachusetts newspaper. In 1882, he moved to New York City and founded Dow Jones & Co. with another reporter Edward Davis Jones.

Dow's Customer's Afternoon Letter sold for two cents each or $5 for a one year subscription.

Chapter 5

Stocks and Domain Names.

Stocks that Own the Best Domain Names

A domain name, or domain for short, is what you type in the web address bar at the top of your web browser. It is usually what comes after the "http://".

For example, WallStreetNewsNetwork.com is a domain name. The interesting thing about these domains is that they can be very valuable. If you had registered some of the one word domains many years ago, you could sell them today for very high prices.

You can still register your own domain name for around $10 to $35 a year, if you can find a good one, but the best ones have been all scooped up, many by publicly traded stocks. Take a look at the following lists.

Stocks that Own the Highest Priced Domain Names

Many large publicly traded corporations understand the value of these domains and have been willing to pay extremely large amounts for certain domains. The following is a list of the highest priced domain names and the names of the stocks that purchased them, along with the purchase price:

fb.com Facebook (FB) $8.5 million

loans.com Bank of America (BAC) $3 million

social.com Salesforce.com (CRM) $2.6 million

mortgage.com Citigroup (C) $1.8 million

fly.com Travelzoo (TZOO) $1.5 million

vista.com Vista Print (VPRT) $1.25 million

mercury.com Hewlett Packard (HPQ) $1.1 million

sky.com British Sky Broadcasting (BSYBF) $1 million

o.co Overstock.co (OSTK) $350 thousand

Sales data came from Domaining.com

Stocks that Own the Shortest Domain Names: One Letter Long

There are very few one-letter domain names that are owned by companies, but generally the companies are stocks that the average investor can own.

The Internet Assigned Numbers Authority put a restriction on single character domains back on December 1, 1993, so if a corporation didn't own the name back then, it would have had to purchase it. Here is a list of one letter domain names and the stocks that own them.

a.co is owned by Amazon.com (AMZN)

g.co is owned by Google (GOOG)

o.co and o.info are both owned by Overstock.com (OSTK).

q.com is owned by CenturyLink (CTL). If you go to q.com, it takes you right to CenturyLink's web site.

x.com is owned by x.commerce, which is owned by eBay (EBAY). When you go to the x.com website, it takes you to the x.commerce website.

y.co is owned by YCO Group Plc, a luxury yacht company. The stock trades on the London Matched Markets Exchange.

z.com is owned by Nissan North America Inc., which is owned by Nissan Motor (NSANY), which trades on NASDAQ. However, the website is currently inactive at the time this was written.

u.tv is owned by UTV Media (UTV.L), a broadcasting and New Media company based in Belfast in Northern Ireland. The company trades on the London Stock Exchange.

Stocks that Own the Best Domain Names

If you can't get a one letter domain, the next best thing is a popular one word domain. If you ever wondered what publicly traded companies have top generic domain names, here are some of the major ones.

asthma.com Glaxosmithkline plc (GSK)

baby.com Johnson & Johnson (JNJ)

book.com Barnes & Noble, Inc. (BKS)

books.com Barnes & Noble, Inc. (BKS)

bras.com Calvin Klein, subsidiary of Phillips-Van Heusen Corporation (PVH)

brew.com Marchex, Inc. (MCHX)

cat.com Caterpillar Inc. (CAT)

construction.com The McGraw-Hill Companies, Inc. (MHP)

flowers.com 1-800-Flowers.com Inc. (FLWS)

flu.com AstraZeneca plc (AZN)

gift.com J. C. Penney Company, Inc (JCP)

help.com CBS Corporation (CBS)

icecream.com Dreyers, division of NESTLE (NSRGY)

jobs.com Monster Worldwide, Inc. (MWW)

lawyers.com LexisNexis, a division of Reed Elsevier NV (ENL) (RUK)

loans.com Bank of America Corporation (BAC)

money.com TimeWarner (TWX)

mortgage.com Citigroup, Inc. (C)

pet.com Petsmart Inc. (PETM)

pets.com Petsmart Inc. (PETM)

realestate.com LendingTree, LLC a division of Tree.com, Inc. (TREE)

school.com Office Depot, Inc. (ODP)

shirt.com owned by Phillips-Van Heusen Corporation (PVH), brings up Amazon.com (AMZN)

shoes.com Brown Shoe Company (BWS)

TV.com CBS (CBS)

underwear.com Calvin Klein, subsidiary of Phillips-Van Heusen Corporation (PVH)

video.com Disney (DIS)

Fred Fuld III

Chapter 6

Crazy Stock Names and Animal Stock Names

It is amazing that there are several publicly traded companies that have strange names. First there is Crazy Woman Creek Bancorp Inc. (CRZY) back in 2007. Crazy Woman is a bank holding company for Buffalo Federal Savings Bank, which serves the Johnson, Campbell, and Sheridan counties in Wyoming.

Speaking of crazy, there is also Crazy Infotech Ltd. (CRAZYINF.BO) which trades on the Bombay Stock Exchange and Crazy Horse Resources (CZH.V) which trades on the Vancouver Stock Exchange. And speaking of horses, there is also Bucking Horse Energy (BUKHF.PK) and Gold Horse International (GHII.OB). And although unicorns are not exactly horses, they look pretty similar. So we have Unicorn Org. (UNICORN.BO) which trades on the Bombay Stock Exchange and Unicorn AIM VCT plc (UAVX.L), traded in London, which is a United Kingdom-based investment management company.

As for other animals, one company has the unusual name of Foley Dog Show Organ (FLDG), and all I could find out about it, besides the fact that it trades on the Pink Sheets, is that it is or was a popular dogs publication company. As for other stocks with dog in the name, there are Blackdog Resources (DOG.V), DogInn, Inc. (DOGI), Guard Dog, Inc. (GRDO), and Bull Dog Sauce Company (BGDSF).

Some stocks that may be the cat's meow include Mad Catz Interactive Inc. (MCZ), which makes accessories for videogame platforms, personal computers, and iPods, Big Cat Energy Corporation (BCTE), which has technology which allows coal bed methane operators to re-inject water produced from productive coal seams, and Storm Cat Energy Corp. (SCUEF).

Let's round out the animal stocks with Cockatoo Coal (CKATF), Cockatoo Ridge Wines (CKTOF), Snake Eyes Golf Clubs (SNKEQ), and finally Coda Octopus Group, Inc. (CDOC), a company which markets underwater technologies and equipment for imaging, mapping, and defense and survey applications.

A stock called Love & Play (56N.F) last traded for 0.002 euros on the Frankfurt Stock Exchange. They operate something called 'Coffee and Stay' shops and erotic products.

Finally, we will end this on a small note with a bank called *the little bank* (LTLB). That's right, the way you see it written is the way it actually is, in all lower case letters, in 'e.e.cummings Style'.

Chapter 7

Highest Priced Shares of Stock

There are actually several stocks that trade above a thousand dollars per share. By the time you read this, there may be more stocks selling over $1,000; then again, there may be fewer. First, every investor and many non-investors, have heard of Warren Buffett's Berkshire Hathaway (BRK-A), which was selling at around $170,000 at the time this book was written. So what about other high flyers?

Historically, there have been stocks that rarely trade, such as Indians Inc. (INDN), which last traded at $30,007 on July 17, 2012. The company owns the Indianapolis Indians, a minor league baseball team which is the second-oldest minor league franchise in American professional baseball. Winter Sports [New] (WSPS), operator of the Whitefish Mountain Resort near Glacier National Park in Montana, which last traded on September 23, 2011 at $30,000.

So let's look at a really high priced stock. Bactolac Pharmaceutical (BTCA) is a company which makes and distributes vitamins, nutraceuticals, and private label nutritional supplements. The stock last traded at $100,000 per share on December 21, 2012. Back in 2008, the stock traded as low as $24,050.

For some strange reason, California seems to have cornered the market in high priced shares, usually bank holding companies. For example, Mechanics Bank (MCHB) currently sells for $13,250. This Richmond, California based bank was founded in 1905.

Farmers & Merchants Bank of Long Beach (FMBL) sells at $5,100 per share. They are based in Long Beach, California. Then there is Sunwest Bank (SWBC), yet another California bank, this one based in Tustin in Orange County. The stock recently closed at an amazing $33,000.

First National Bank Alaska (FBAK) is another west coast bank, this one based a little farther north in Anchorage, Alaska. The stock recently sold at $1,751. American Bank Holdings Inc. (ABKH), which operates in Washington, DC, sells for $3,900. Acap Corp. (ACPC), a life insurance holding company, recently sold at $2,900 a share.

Ergo Science Corporation (ERGN) is a publisher of business information through printed magazines, Web sites, data services and directories. The stock last traded at $8,000.

A.D. Makepeace Company (MAKE) is a Massachusetts based cranberry grower in the towns of Carver, Middleborough, Plymouth, Rochester, and Wareham. It last traded at $5,900 on September 30, 2013. The company was founded in 1922.

Highwater Ethanol LLC (HEOL) last traded at $5,000 per share on September 13, 2013.

The Seibels Bruce Group (SBBG) is a provider of services to the insurance industry and offers automobile, flood, and other property and casualty insurance services. This stock also last traded at $5,000 a share on September 23, 2013.

Seaboard Corp. (SEB), which trades on the New York Stock Exchange, is in the business of food processing and ocean transportation, and their stock sells for $2,713.

LICT Corporation (LICT) trades at $2,488. The company is a provider of broadband and communication services.

Did a Stock Really Trade for Over $1,000,000 a Share?

What do you think was the highest priced share of stock ever to trade? And what do you think that share price was? If you think it's Warren Buffett's Berkshire Hathaway (BRK-A) (BRK-B), you would be wrong.

The company was Yahoo! Japan Corporation (YAHOY) (YAHOF), according to StockMarketTrivia.com. The Shareholder Relations Representative for the Yahoo! Japan company told me that the highest price of the stock was 167.9 million Japanese Yen on Feb.

22, 2000. If you exchange the amount of Japanese Yen into US dollars at the exchange rate at that time (Approx USD1=JPY111.01), it was approximately $1,512,500 per share.

Yahoo! Japan is a Japanese Internet company formed as a joint venture between the American internet company Yahoo! (YHOO) and the Japanese internet company SoftBank (SFTBF). It was founded in 1996 and is headquartered in Tokyo, Japan.

The stock trades on the JASDAQ and in the US in the over-the-counter market.

Chapter 8

Vanity Stock Ticker Symbols of Wall Street

A stock symbol, also known as a stock ticker, is the abbreviation used for company names that are used to look up prices of stocks. The term "stock ticker" comes from the names of the machines that were used in the old days to print out the prices of stocks on a ticker tape, a long thin strip of paper.

One way that a publicly traded company can get attention is by having an unusual symbol, especially if it spells a word that relates to their business. In other words, not just a company abbreviation such as YHOO for Yahoo, or GOOG for Google, or DELL for Dell, or EBAY for eBay. And not just the company's initials, such as IBM for International Business Machines.

An example of a great symbol is NUT, the former symbol for ML Macadamia Orchards, a macadamia nut farming company in Hawaii that trades on the New York Stock Exchange. The letters of the symbol are not the same as the initials for the company, yet the symbol tells you right away what the business is.

Another great symbol is GAS for AGL Resources Inc. In case you haven't guessed what business AGL is in, it is a distributor of natural gas.

The following is a list of Vanity Stock Ticker Symbols™ for a group of stocks from 1990. These are the actual stock symbols for these corporations at that time. Cover up the names of the companies with your hand and see if you can guess what kind of business they were in.

BABY	Fertility & Genetic Resources
BEAM	Summit Technology Incorporated
BLMP	Airship Intl. Ltd.
BLUD	Immucor Incorporated
BOOK	Village Green Bookstore Incorporated
BOOM	Explosive Fabricators Incorporated
BRAU	Pavichevich Brewing Corporation
BSBL	Score Board Incorporated
BUCS	American Franchise Group Incorporated
BURN	Trilling Medical Technology Incorporated
BYTE	Compu Com Systems Incorporated
CARS	US Cargo Incorporated
CGUL	Margate Ventures Incorporated
CHIK	Golden Poultry Co. Incorporated
COLD	Texas American Group Incorporated
DINE	Mascott Corporation
DOSE	Choice Drug Systems Incorporated
DRNK	Cable Car Beverage Corporation
EARS	Hearx Ltd.
FAIR	Renaissance Entertainment Corporation
FAME	Flame master Corporation
FAXM	Hotelcopy Incorporated
FLAG	First Federal Savings Bank of La Grange
FOIL	Forest Oil Corporation
FONE	Farmstead Telephone Group
FOTO	Seattle Filmworks Incorporated
FUEL	Griffith Consumers Corporation
FUN	Cedar Fair, L.P.
FUSE	First United Savings Bank FSB
GAIT	Langen Biomechanics Group
GARD	Denning Mobile Robotics
GEMS	Electronic Spec. Products Incorporated
GGGG	4 G Data Systems Incorporated
GOGO	Nutri-Products Incorporated

GONE	Plastigone Technology Incorporated.
GRIT	Grubb & Ellis Realty Incorporated Trust
HIRE	Diversified Human Resources Group
JAIL	Adtec. Incorporated
JOIN	Jones Inter Cable Incorporated
KDNY	Home Intensive Care
KIDS	Magic Years Child Care Center
KIDZ	Direct Connect International
KITS	Meridian Diagnostics Incorporated
KRUZ	Europa Cruises Corporation
LABL	Multi-Color Corporation
LADY	Tennis Lady Incorporated
LAMP	S.O.I. Ind. Incorporated
LENS	Concord Camera Corporation
LENZ	Vision Sciences Incorporated
LIPSA	Showcase Cosmetics Incorporated
LOAN	Surety Capital Corporation
LUBE	Auto Spa Corporation
LUNG	L A Blockers Incorporated
LUVSW	Southwest Airlines 90 Warrants
MALL	Auto Spa Automalls Incorporated
MAME	Mobile America Corporation
MEMRY	Ramtron Australia Ltd.
MOLE	Flowmole Corporation
NASA	North American Savings Association
NOIZ	Micronetics Incorporated
OUCH	Occupational-Urgent Care
PIZA	National Pizza Corporation
PLAY	Players Intl. Incoroorated
PLUG	Component Guard Incorporated
POPI	Fast Food Operators
PTA	Career Com Corporation
PULP	Kingston Systems Incorporated
QPON	Seven Oaks Intl. Incorporated
READ	American Learning Corporation
REAL	Reliability Incorporated
REFR	Research Frontiers
RELY	Ingres Corporation
RITE	Trvlsys Incorporated

RRRC	Tri-R Systems Corporation
SEED B	DeKalb Genetics Corporation Class B
SHIP	Regency Cruises Incorporated
SHOE	Millfeld Trading Co. Inc.
SKIL	Canterbury Educational Services
SODA	A&W Brands Incorporated
STAG	Security Tag System Incorporated
TAPE	Magnetech Corporation
TONE	One Bancorp.
TOOL	Easco Band Tools Incorporated
TREE	Aspen Leaf Incorporated
TSTM	Media Logic Incorporated
TUXX	Al's Formal Wear Incorporated
UEAT	Restaurant Hotline Systems Incorporated
WCTV	Wescott Communications Incorporated.
WHEL	Roadmaster Industries Incorporated
YUMY	Tofruzen Incorporated

Now here are a few current symbols. See if you can guess the companies, and if you can't guess that, see if you can guess the businesses these companies are in.

CAFE   iPath Pure Beta Coffee ETN, a coffee future ETN

CAKE   Cheesecake Factory Incorporated, restaurant chain

EGOV   NIC, Inc., online services that enable governments use the Internet

FUEL   Rocket Fuel Inc., an artificial-intelligence digital advertising

FUND   Royce Focus Trust, Inc. a diversified, closed-end investment company.

GROW   U.S. Global Investors, Inc., mutual fund management services

KOOL   ThermoGenesis Corp., automated blood processing systems

LABL   Multi-Color Corporation, supplier of decorative label solutions

PAY   Veriphone Holdings, Inc., secure electronic payment transactions

PZZA   Papa John's International, Inc., pizza delivery and carryout restaurants

ROCK   Gibraltar Industries, Inc., distributor of residential and commercial building products

SEED   Origin Agritech Limited, distribution of hybrid crop seeds in China

TAP   Molson Coors Brewing Company, beer distributor

XRAY   Dentsply International, Inc., products for the dental market.

OO

Up until 2007 when Oakley, Inc. was taken over by Luxottica, Oakley had the symbol OO. The company designs, manufactures, and sells sunglasses, prescription eyewear, and goggles.

Trivia Question:

Why did Oakley choose that symbol?

Trivia Answer:

The two O's next to each other is an emoticon for eyeglasses.

SCAM

Can you guess what company has the stock symbol SCAM? Actually, it is usually published as SCAM.L as it trades on the London Stock Exchange. It is a highly regarded British mutual fund. It certainly has an easy stock symbol to remember.

HOG

Can the Stock Symbol Affect the Stock Price?

Is having an interesting stock symbol just that, interesting? Or is it possible value can be added to the stock by having a great stock symbol. Let's look at one example which is interesting trivia in itself.

For many years, the stock symbol for Harley Davidson (HOG) was HDI. However on August 15, 2006, the company changed its symbol to HOG, which is a term that is closely associated with Harley, and is also the abbreviation for the Harley Owners Group. If we look t the performance of the stock for the five months previous to the symbol change from May 15 to August 15, the stock was up only 14.7%; however for the five months subsequent to the stock symbol change, the stock was up 28.3%, almost double the return.

One Letter Stock Symbols

One letter stock tickers are very hard for corporations to get. Remember, there are only 26 possible ones and most of them are taken. Here they are:

A   Agilent Technologies Inc.
B   Barnes Group Inc.
C   Citigroup, Inc.
D   Dominion Resources, Inc.
E   Eni SpA
F   Ford Motor Co.
G   Genpact Ltd.
H   Hyatt Hotels Corporation
I   Intelsat S.A.
J   available
K   Kellogg Company
L   Loews Corporation
M   Macy's, Inc.
N   NetSuite Inc.
O   Realty Income Corp.
P   Pandora Media, Inc.
Q   Quintiles Transnational Holdings Inc.
R   Ryder System, Inc.
S   Sprint Corporation
T   AT&T, Inc.
U   available
V   Visa Inc.
W   available
X   United States Steel Corp.
Y   Alleghany Corporation
Z   Zillow, Inc.

Fred Fuld III

Chapter 9

First Bond Broker &
the First Stock Broker

History: How did it begin?

In order to have stocks, you need to have ownership of businesses. A stock can be defined as a share of ownership of a company or business, which can be bought or sold. The word stock also refers to the certificate or document representing shares of ownership of a company.

Back in the period of 9000 BC to 8000 BC, shepherds used tokens made out of clay for accounting purposes. Unfortunately, since writing hadn't been invented at that time, there is no way to know whether shares of ownership existed at that time, or even businesses as we know it even existed.

From 4000 BC to 3000 BC a clay purse called a bulla was used to hold accounting tokens. The bullas were completely sealed, but could always be broken open in the event of a discrepancy on a transaction. Seals were imprinted on the bullas, then later written notations used, and these inscriptions led to what eventually become what is called cuneiform.

During the period of 2500 BC to 1800 BC, cuneiform was used extensively. Cuneiform was created by using a reed as a stylus to make impressions on clay tablets, while the tablets were wet. The tablets were then dried either in the sun or in ovens. Cuneiform was used for financial transactions, business documents, and religious writings in Babylon and throughout the area of Mesopotamia. There was extensive economic activity going on at this time including agriculture, ranching, trading, fishing, and shipping.

First Bond Transactions

When looking for the first bond transaction, it is necessary to define what a bond is. A bond is a loan to a business in which the business agrees to pay back the loan to the investor within a certain period of time and incur a certain interest rate. In addition, the loan should be documented transferable; in other words, it can be bought and sold like an investment. The first bond transaction, which has actually been documented by cuneiform, involved the lending of silver to a business, and that loan was then sold to another individual.

According to Professor William N. Goetzmann, author of the *Financing Civilization* website and the book that he co-edited, *The Origins of Value*, the City of Ur, located in Mesopotamia, was the first documented city with a financial district, and had a thriving economy. The ruins of the city were excavated by Sir Leonard Woolley during the 1920's. Later, Professor Marc Van De Mieroop of Columbia University researched and cataloged the discovered clay tablets, which were documented in his book, *Society and Enterprise in Old Babylonian Ur*. He even found an area which could be considered the financial district of Ur with a significant number of cuneiform tablets documenting numerous financial transactions around 1800 BC.

Goetzmann's book, which is a fascinating study of financial history especially ancient financial history, discusses how a gentleman by the name of Dumuzi-gamil was the largest financier in Ur. Dumuzi-gamil was primarily in the bakery business, but in addition to being an entrepreneur, he was also an investor and trader. One of his techniques was "borrowing low and lending high".

At that time, the rulers had restrictions on the amount of interest that can be charged, setting a cap at 20% no matter how long or short the loan. This was 20% total, not 20% per year. The government didn't regulate the length of time for a loan.

So what did Dumuzi-gamil do? He borrowed silver at as low an interest rate that he could negotiate for five years (because he was such a good credit risk, he could borrow at much less than 20%), and loaned it out, in much smaller amounts, to individuals and businesses, at 20% for one to three months.

So here was the first bond transaction. In 1796 BC, Shumi-abum (who might be considered the first bond broker), loaned 250 grams of silver to Dumuzi-gamil for a period of five years. Dumuzi-gamil agreed to return a somewhat greater amount at the end of that time frame. After the loan was made, the loan or "bond" was immediately sold to two investors. Fortunately for the two investors, Dumuzi-gamil paid the loan off in full with interest in 1791 BC. This was all documented on a cuneiform tablet, which could be considered the bond certificate.

First "Stockbroker"

First "stockbroker" might be considered to be Ea-nasir who financed shipping expeditions to Dilmun. Dilmun was a major trading community in the ancient world, located in the islands around what is now known as Bahrain.

According to Professor Goetzmann, Ea-nasir set up an investment in a trading expedition, and collected silver from a group of investors, both large and small. The investors could receive an unlimited return on their investments and their loss would be limited to the amount of their investment, similar to a corporation. (In other words, if the boat sank, they wouldn't have to contribute additional funds to cover the cost of the boat or to buy a new one.) The investment return came back in the form of gems, copper and other items, which the Dilmun traders gave in return for the silver.

First Financial "Crash"

The first financial crash took place in 1788 BC. The ruler at the time, King Rim-Sin, voided all loans, causing the lenders to be wiped out.

Readers who are interested in exploring ancient financial history further should check out Goetzmann's book, which I highly recommend.

Financial Cuneiform

Chapter 10

Miscellaneous Trivia

According to Footnoted.org, back in 2007, the former SEC Chairman Arthur Levitt used to sell his old ties on eBay (EBAY). However, his staff members would find and buy his ties off of eBay and wear them in to work as a joke.

What corporation has increased their annual dividend from $845.76 in 2005 to $1106.96 in 2006, has paid dividends since 1982, and no investment is required to receive this dividend?
Note:
This is a trick question.
Answer:
The Alaska Permanent Fund Corporation

Did You know that One Pound equals 490 U.S. Dollars?
Yes, 490 dollars equals one pound (that's a pound in weight, not British pounds). That's right, if you stack 490 dollar bills on a scale, they will weight one pound, according to the Bank Note Reporter.

What has been the longest-listed company on the NYSE?
Con Edison, which was listed in 1824 as the New York Gas Light Company

What was the oldest company that was listed on the NYSE?
Bowne & Company, Inc. It was founded 1775 but it wasn't listed until 1999.

What New York Stock Exchange Member has the longest service membership?
David Granger, who has been a member since 1926, for 76 years.

When did the Dow Jones Industrial Average first close over 100?
January 12, 1906, when it closed at 100.25

When did stock share trading volume for the NYSE first go over 1 million?
1886

When did stock share trading volume for the NYSE first go over 10 million?
1929

When did stock share trading volume for the NYSE first go over 1 billion?
1997

What stock had GRRR for its stock symbol?
Lion Country Safari, a drive through zoo

What was the original name of the American Stock Exchange and why?
The Curb, because it was originally started by traders on the streets of New York City standing on and by the curb.

Was there really a stock exchange in Hawaii?
Yes, the Honolulu Stock Exchange operated from 1910 to 1976.

 Is there really a stock that owns a brothel?
Yes, a company called Planet Platinum Ltd. (PNNFF) owns the Daily Planet, a licensed brothel in Melbourne, Australia. Well technically, the company owns the building that the brothel is housed in, not the actual business. The stock trades on the Australian Securities Exchange and over-the-counter in the US.

Chapter 11

What is the Smallest Stock Exchange in the World?

If you measure stock exchanges by how many stocks they have listed, the smallest stock exchange in the world is the Douala Stock Exchange also known as the DSX, based in Cameroon.

Cameroon is located on the western coast of the African continent. The country has a population of a little over 20.5 million.

Cameroon's stock exchange has had only one listing since its founding in 2001, Société des Eaux Minérales du Cameroun (SEMC). However, in May of 2008, they added their second issue, Société Africaine Forestière et Agricole du Cameroun (SAFACAM). The exchange also trades government bonds, however those are considered unlisted securities.

Chapter 12

The First Medical Marijuana Stock

It may be hard to believe but there is actually a publicly traded company that has been selling marijuana for many years. Actually, a marijuana extract (tetrahydrocannabinol). Unimed Pharmaceuticals Inc. (formerly Unimed Inc. until they changed their name in June of 1994), a U.S company originally based in Buffalo Creek, Illinois, that used to be publicly traded, manufactures Marinol (also known as Dronabinol), which is a marijuana extract used as an appetite stimulant and anti-emetic.) The drug was approved by the FDA for treatment of anorexia associated with weight loss in patients with AIDS; and nausea and vomiting associated with cancer chemotherapy in patients who have failed to respond adequately to conventional anti-emetic treatments and for treating AIDS wasting syndrome. The company received approval for their drug on May 31, 1985 with dosages of 2.5, 5. and 10 milligrams.

The company had over 6,100,000 shares outstanding and during the early 1990's, the stock traded between $2 per share up to a high of $11 3/4 per share. They ended up the end of 1994 at a price of $2 1/2 per share bid price. Unimed was taken over by Solvay Pharmaceuticals, which is a publicly traded company based in Brussels, Belgium. The company's stock is traded in Europe and also its ADR's are traded in the U. S. Over-the-Counter market with the symbol SVYZY.

Chapter 13

Biggest Percentage Gainer in One Day

There may be many stocks that have gone up several thousand percent in one day, especially the ones that sell for pennies or sub-pennies a share. And it is difficult to find such data. However, I accidentally stumbled upon one that was up an unbelievably huge amount.

If you looked at Kbridge Energy Corp. (BMMCF) on Yahoo! Finance on Tuesday, August 27, 2013, near the end of the trading day, you would have seen that the stock was up 259,934.34% for the day. (Other sources confirmed this percentage increase.)

The previous close was $0.0002 per share, and it had jumped up to $0.52 per share. In other words, if you had invested $100 in the stock to buy 500,000 shares, it would have become $260,000. The stock actually got as high as 94 cents that day but ended up closing at 29 cents a share.

The company is a broker for energy and resource related contracts in South Korea. It is based in Las Vegas, Nevada, and is a development stage company which was founded in 2002.

Chapter 14

Billionaires & Show Business: What Billionaire Investor Appeared on a Soap Opera

Here is a trivia question for you. What billionaire investor appeared as himself on a soap opera?

Hint number 1: The Soap Opera is *All My Children*

Hint number 2: This billionaire appeared not once but twice in this TV series

Hint number 3: He plays himself in this show

Hint number 4: He also played the part of James Madison in an animated TV series called *Liberty's Kids: Est. 1776*

Give up? Who else but Warren Buffett. He appeared in the *All My Children* Episode 9869 on May 8, 2008 and Episode 9870 on May 9, 2008. He has also appeared in five documentaries.

Chapter 15

Microsoft and the Celebrity Game Show Business?

It may be hard to believe, but it looks like Microsoft (MSFT) may have tried to get into the celebrity game show business a few years ago. They were so serious about it that they even filed a patent on their idea, patent number 6,800,031 filed on April 15, 2002.

Here is the abstract:

"An interaction competition provides an entertaining enjoyable environment for a player to compete against a celebrity in a head-to-head trivia game. The questions may be associated with the celebrity rather than random general information or general trivia. The celebrity can participate via prerecorded audio media, prerecorded audio-visual media, or in a live real-time format. A goal of the competition is for a player to gain more points than the celebrity. Another goal of the competition is for the player to answer more questions correctly than the celebrity. At least one or more game episodes can be provided on computer-readable media. A game episode may be implemented with a product featuring a celebrity. The competition can be provided in many different gaming environments. The competition can be provided online via a web-based format; a television game show format; telephone call-in radio talk show format; or a cellular phone game format."

.

Chapter 16

Warren Buffett Trivia

Do you know everything that there is to know about Warren Buffett, the billionaire head of Berkshire Hathaway?

1. Warren Buffett's father was a republican congressman.

2. Warren Buffett is of Huguenot ancestry.

3. His first stock purchase was three shares of Cities Service Preferred purchased when he was eleven years old.

4. When he was fourteen years old, he filed his first tax return, which listed his watch and bicycle as a tax deduction of $35 for his paper route.

5. He was a capitalist at a very young age, not only delivering newspapers, but selling magazine subscriptions door-to-door, selling golf balls, and selling Coca-Cola (KO).

6. He owned a chain of pinball machines in various barber shops when he was fifteen years old.

7. In his high school yearbook, under his picture, it says 'likes math; a future stock broker.'

8. He received his B.S. in Economics from the University of Nebraska–Lincoln when he was only 19 years old.

9. He paid $31,500 for the Omaha house he lives in today (although he bought it 52 years ago).

10. He owns a house in Laguna Beach, California

11. Buffett attended Columbia Business School because Benjamin Graham and David Dodd taught there.

12. In 1951, he received a M.S. in Economics from Columbia Business School.

13. He made almost $10,000 by the age of 20 in 1950.

14. Buffett's father and Benjamin Graham told him not to work on Wall Street.

15. He taught a night class at the University of Nebraska-Omaha called Investment Principals.

16. He owned a Sinclair Texaco gas station in his early 20's.

17. His starting salary at Benjamin Graham's company was $12,000 a year.

18. When he was 26 years old, he had $174,000 in savings.

19. He became a millionaire in 1962.

20. Buffett first bought Berkshire Hathaway stock at $7.60 per share.

Chapter 17

The CIA Hedge Fund

Did you know that back in 1999, the CIA (yes the US government's Central Intelligence Agency) set up its own venture capital fund? The fund, called In-Q-Tel, has invested in over 100 companies.

It even invested in the technology that is now known as Google Earth, according to the book, *Wave Theory For Alternative Investments: Riding The Wave with Hedge Funds, Commodities, and Venture Capital* by Stephen Todd Walker.

Fred Fuld III

Chapter 18

What are PINES and QUIBS and PDs

      Minibonds™ are very low priced bond. These are bonds that are traded just like stocks on the New York Stock Exchange or American Stock Exchange for around $25 per share. They are almost like preferred stocks except that they pay interest instead of dividends and they usually have a specific maturity date.

      Sometimes they are referred to as PINES (Public Income Notes) or QUIBS (Quarterly Interest Bonds) or QUICS (Quarterly Income Capital Securities) or QUIDS (Quarterly Income Debt Securities). There are even a few that are issued as Perpetual Debt, which means that there is no maturity date.

Chapter 19

Stock Market Firsts

When were the first stock tickers and ticker tapes used?

1867

What was the first firm that was a member of the NYSE that became listed on the NYSE?

Merrill Lynch, which became listed on July 27, 1971.

What was the first widely owned stock?

The first widely owned stock was the Dutch East India Company, which was founded in 1602. It was the largest company for a couple of centuries. It financed trade expeditions for such items as spices, silk, precious stones, porcelain, and cloves.

What was the first listed company on the New York Stock Exchange?

Bank of New York, which was the first corporate stock traded under the Buttonwood tree in 1792, and the first listed company on the NYSE.

Who was the first African American member of the NYSE?

Joseph L. Searles III, who became a member on February 12, 1970

Who was the first female member of the NYSE?

Muriel Siebert, who became a member on December 28, 1967

Who was the first woman member who worked on the trading floor on a regular basis of the NYSE?

Alice Jarcho, became a member on Oct. 14, 1976, began working on the trading floor on October 28, 1976

What was the first African American owned NYSE member firm?

Daniels & Bell Inc., in 1971

What were the first publicly traded securities in the U.S.?

$80 million in U.S. Government bonds that were issued in 1790 to refinance Revolutionary War debt.

When where the beginnings of the New York Stock Exchange established and what was the name of the founding document?

In 1792, the Buttonwood Agreement, signed by twenty-four brokers and merchants on Wall Street, agreeing to trade securities on a common commission basis.

What was the first listed company on the New York Stock Exchange?

Bank of New York, which was the first corporate stock traded under the Buttonwood tree in 1792, and the first listed company on the NYSE.

Chapter 20

The First Stock Exchanges

According to some sources, stock exchanges originally came about from trading in agricultural and other commodities during the Middle Ages at what were called Euro-Fairs. Credit was commonly given, and therefore supporting documents were created such as drafts, notes, and bills of exchange. These documents were traded by the merchants, and it is believed that it is the origin of the term "Merchant Banker."

These were the precursors to modern stock and bond certificates. During the seventeenth century, certificates of ownership of businesses came into existence. These businesses were primarily involved in trade with the East Indies.

What were the five oldest stock exchanges worldwide?
Antwerp Bourse 1460
Lyons Bourse 1506
Toulouse Bourse 1549
Hamburg Bourse 1558
London Royal Exchange 1571

What were the three oldest stock exchanges in the United States?
Philadelphia Stock Exchange 1790
New York Stock Exchange 1792
Boston Stock Exchange 1834

What were the three oldest commodities exchanges in the US?
Chicago Board of Trade 1848
Kansas City Board of Trade 1856
New York Cotton Exchange 1870

Philadelphia Stock Exchange
The First Stock Exchange in the United States

Chapter 21

Stock and Bond Certificates

What was the oldest stock certificate?
The oldest company for which a stock certificate exists was dated 1299. It was issued for a Swedish company called Stora-Kopparberg. The company is still in existence and is now known as Stora Enso. It is involved in the forestry and mining industry.

What was the highest denomination for any stock certificate worldwide?
5 billion marks (5,000,000,000) par value for the German company Croning-Schloss AG in 1923.

What was the smallest US bond in physical size?
The State of Louisiana 'Baby Bond' Certificate, called a Baby Bond for three reasons: Its small denomination of $5 (making this the lowest denomination US municipal bond also), its small size of about 3 inches by 4.25 inches (8 cm by 11 cm) excluding coupons, and its vignette of a baby wearing a hat. (See more details in the Weird Words of Wall Street section in the last part of the book.)

What was the largest physical size of a bond on one piece of paper?
New York Cable Railway, which measures almost 2 feet by 3 feet including coupons, issued as a $1000 denomination and dated 1884.

What was the highest denomination for a U. S. railroad bond?
$42,110,000 for the New York Central & Hudson River Railroad (Rail Road) Co. Bond, 100-yr, 4.5%, registered gold, dated 1913, due 2013, 'Series A,' , refunding & improvement issue.

What was the lowest denomination for a railroad bond?
$2 for the Ferrocarriles Nacionales de Mexico (Mexico) Bond, 3-yr, 6%, gold note, 1914, due 1917, denominated in gold US dollars, Mexican gold pesos (4 Pesos), pounds and Reich marks, Series B.

Chapter 22

The First Woman Stockbroker

Who was the First Woman Stockbroker?

Hint: She was Also the First Woman Presidential Candidate

Victoria Claflin Woodhull, also known as Victoria Claflin, Victoria Woodhull, and Victoria Woodhull Martin, was born in 1838 to very poor parents in the backwoods of western Ohio. Her father, Reuben Buckman Claflin, had run-ins with the law and her mother, Roxanna Hummel Claflin, was considered to be a mystic.

Victoria Woodhull was a stockbroker, and with her younger sister, Tennessee " Tennie" Claflin, started the first woman-owned stock brokerage firm in New York City. She was also a strong proponent of women's rights and even became a candidate for president of the United States, with abolitionist leader and former slave Frederick Douglass as her running mate.

At the age of 15, Victoria married a man named Dr. Canning Woodhull, who was twelve years her senior and supposedly a physician. She took his last name and was known by that name for much of her life, even though she subsequently married Colonel James H. Blood eight years later.

In 1869, Victoria & Tennessee moved to New York, and a year later, started the investment firm, Woodhull, Claflin & Company. The women were able to set up and maintain their firm through the help of Commodore Vanderbilt, a railroad industrialist who was one of the richest people in American history.

Apparently, Vanderbilt didn't care for doctors, because they couldn't cure his health ailments. However, he did have an interest in mediums, so he ended up making an appointment with Tennessee, who claimed to generate electricity with her hands and could help prolong his life. She was in her twenties at the time, and Vanderbilt was in his seventies. He saw Tennessee every day, and reportedly planned to marry her. However, his family talked him out of it.

In regards to the brokerage firm, it hit the newspaper headlines in early 1870, causing men and women to line up to invest with them.

Victoria Woodhull later became a strong proponent of women's rights and ran for president on the Equal Rights Party (also known as the People's Party) ticket. Frederick Douglass was her running mate, although he didn't campaign. Ulysses S. Grant won the election, and Woodhull came in ninth place, garnering less than 0.1% of the popular vote. (Remember, women couldn't vote in those days.)

Picture is that of Tennessee Claflin - Library of Congress

Chapter 23

Early Investment Bubbles

Tulip Mania

In 1593, Holland was introduced to the first tulip bulbs that came from Constantinople. The popularity of the bulbs began to increase, and by 1610, bulbs were used as dowries for brides.

Then in 1634, the Dutch middle class started to buy tulip bulbs, causing them to become status symbols. The following year, a single bulb sold for $76,000, and in 1636, the bulbs began trading on the Amsterdam stock exchange.

In 1637, the glow was off the bulbs, and investors started to sell. Prices eventually tanked by 90% in 6 weeks!!!

Fred Fuld III

South Sea Bubble

"I can calculate the movement of the stars, but NOT the madness of men." - Sir Isaac Newton, after losing a fortune (£20,000) in the bubble

In 1711, the British government was in debt to the tune of £ 10,000,000. A group of merchants got together and bought the debt in return for being given exclusive trading rights in South America, primarily the countries of Chile & Peru.

These merchants then created the South Sea Trading Company to take advantage of these trading rights. The shares of stock in the company became very popular, with prices rising from £100 to £1000 per share in less than one year.

Other businesses started up from all the frenzy of the stock South Sea increase. (Remind you of the dot com boom?) The following is a list of some of the unusual businesses of startups that raised money at the time. The list comes from the book *Extraordinary Popular Delusions and the Madness of Crowds* by Charles MacKay.

Trading in hair
Manufacturing square cannon balls
Perpetual motion wheel
Importing walnut-trees from Virginia
Extracting silver from lead
"Carrying on an undertaking of great advantage" without telling you exactly what they would do with your money

In actuality, the company's profits were minimal. Then in September of 1720, investors stopped buying the South Sea stock and most of the stocks of other companies. Of course, the South Sea stock finally collapsed.

Even though no security laws existed at that time, Lord Molesworth, who was a Parliament member, recommended that "the South-Sea Company directors be tied in sacks, and thrown into the Thames"

Mississippi Company

The Mississippi Company was started by Scottish businessman John Law in 1717. It was established to trade with the French Colonies of North America including Louisiana. The company had a 20 year monopoly with the French government.

Law had an unusual way of promoting his company's stock. His advertising stated that Louisiana is filled with mountains of gold and silver. He also promised a 40% dividend.

From 1719 to 1720, the company's shares rose from 500 to 15,000 livres in France, a return of 2900%.

According to the Extraordinary Popular Delusions book:

"The Rue de Quincampoix was the grand resort of the jobbers, and it being a narrow, inconvenient street, accidents continually occurred in it, from the tremendous pressure of the crowd.

Houses in it, worth, in ordinary times, a thousand livres of yearly rent, yielded as much as twelve or sixteen thousand. A cobbler, who had a stall in it, gained about two hundred livres a day by letting it out, and furnishing writing materials to brokers and their clients.

A hunchbacked man who stood in the street gained considerable sums by lending his hump as a writing-desk to the eager speculators!

At nightfall, it was often found necessary to send a troop of soldiers to clear the street."

Getting shares from Law was the primary goal of many investors. Some aristocrats waited six hours to see him, and bribes paid to Law's servants.

Many people were poor in the morning, and went to bed wealthy. Mortimer wrote about how a wealthy man told his servant to go out and sell 250 shares for him. The master asked that he sell the shares for 8,000 livres per share, but the servant actually sold them for 10,000 livres per share. This was a difference of 500,000 livres which was pocketed by servant. There was no additional documentation about what the servant later did, but I'm sure he retired.

Like all bubbles, this one didn't last. In 1721, the shares dropped back to 500 livres, with a 97% decline in the market capitalization by the end of 1721.

So Law fled France and went to Venice, with no money and no jewelry, but had one diamond with him. By 1729, he died of pneumonia, a pauper.

Chapter 24

Where Did the Term Ponzi Scheme Come From?

"Even if they never got anything for it, it was cheap at that price. Without malice aforethought I had given them the best show that was ever staged in their territory since the landing of the Pilgrims! It was easily worth fifteen million bucks to watch me put the thing over!" ~ Charles Ponzi, from an interview at Ponzi's deathbed

Charles Ponzi was born in Lugo, Italy in 1882. He was known by several names and his aliases included Charles Ponei, Charles P. Bianchi, Carl Ponzi, and Carlo Ponzi. He stood 5 feet 2 inches tall. Ponzi's first job was as a postal worker in Italy.

After dropping out of the University of Rome, he took the SS Vancouver to Boston, Massachusetts in 1903 arriving with only $2.50 in his pocket. When he arrived, he learned to speak and read English.

Ponzi had several run-ins with the law, and served some jail time. He later started a large directory advertising business (somewhat similar to the coupons books you receive in the mail.) His directory company went out of business, but he did receive a letter from Spain asking about his catalog, and in the envelope was enclosed a Postal Reply Coupon, something he had never seen.

These coupons could be purchased in one country, sent to someone in another company, and the recipient could redemm them in their own country for their own country's postage.

Ponzi discovered that Postal Reply Coupons could be purchased in Europe for about one cent in American funds, due to favorable exchange rates, and could be cashed in for six cents worth of United States stamps

He decided to set up a company to take advantage of this profitable transaction. He promoted his business to friends and associates, claiming net profits of 400% after all expenses. He then promised a 50% return to investors in 45 days or 100% return if investors were willing to wait in 90 days

He started a company called the Securities Exchange Company, which is sort of strange as it is very similar to the name of the government agency, the Securities and Exchange Commission.

As word spread, he began hiring salesmen, and paid large commissions. In February of 1920, he raised $5,000. By the following month, he had raised $30,000. Then in May, investments were up to $420,000.

The money that was raised was kept in Hanover Trust Bank. Ponzi was hoping to take control of it, since by July 1920, he had millions deposited there.

Ponzi survived one attempted run on the company and an investigation by the state of Massachusetts. However, Clarence Barron, publisher of Barron's, did an investigation of Ponzi and discovered that there would have to be 160 million postal reply coupons would have to be in circulation for the company business to work, yet the U. S. Post Office said that only 27,000 were in circulation. This caused a second run on the company.

Eventually, the company was raided by Federal Agents who shut the company down, along with Hanover Trust Bank. Ponzi was arrested on August 13, 1920, and was sent to prison. He died a pauper.

Chapter 25

Investment Jokes, Wall Street Jokes, and Stock Market Jokes

I wanted to create a little investment humor so I created all these jokes myself. If you don't find them funny, then just continue on to the next chapter.

Broker: What you become after investing in dot com stocks.

Bull: What comes out of your stockbroker's mouth.

Bear: What your brokerage account becomes after investing in Enron.

Short: What you end up being after shorting stocks in your portfolio.

Bond: A thing you used to have between you and your stockbroker before he lost your money.

Call: What a stockbroker does when he has a hot tip for you.

Tip: What you won't be leaving your waiter, if you invest based on his hot stock ideas.

Over the Counter: Where you'll be getting your food from when you go out to dinner, after losing your money in the stock market.

Volume: What you turn up on the radio when the financial report comes on.

Funny Mergers

These are the names that would result if the following publicly traded companies were to become involved in a merger.

If the following companies were to merge: Caterpillar, Gottschalks, Uranium Energy, Tongjitang Chinese Medicines, you would end up with **Cat Gott Ur Tong**.

Du Pont, YouBet.com, Bell Industries, Even Technologies, Magic Software Enterprises = **Du, You, Bell, Even, Magic**

Honeywell and Dewey Electronics = **Honey Dew**

Agfeed Industries, Pfizer, Fortune Brands, Fomento Econmico Mexicano = **Fee, Pfi, Fo, Fom**

Exxon Mobil, Markel Corp., The9 Limited, Spotlight Homes = **Ex, Mark, The, Spot**

Harken Energy, Herald Resources, Fallen Angels Income Fund and Singapore Fund = **Hark, the Herald, Angels, Sing**

Deckers Outdoor Corp., The9 Limited, Hallmark Financial Services = **Deck, The, Hall**

Apple Inc., Omega Navigation Enterprises, Intel = **Apple, Ome, I.**

Harken Energy (HKN) + Herald National Bank (HNB) + Fallen Angels Income Fund (FAINX) + Singapore Fund (SGF) = **Hark, Herald, Angels, Sing**

Deckers Outdoor Corp. (DECK) + The 9 Limited (NCTY) + Hallmark Financial Services (HALL) = **Deck, The, Hall**

Little Bank Inc. (LTLB.OB) + Towne Bank (TOWN) + Bethlehem Steel = **Little, Towne, Bethlehem**

Joy Global (JOY) + Two Harbors Investment Corp. (TWO) + The World Series of Golf, Inc. (WSGF.PK) = **Joy, Two, The World**

* * *

So a woman went to her doctor to find out the results of her tests, and the doctor said, "I'm sorry, but you only have six months to live."

The woman said, "What can be done?"

He replied, "I'm sorry, there is no cure and nothing that can be done."

The woman said, "Oh doctor, there has to be something I can do."

And the doctor said, "Marry a stockbroker; it will be the longest six months of you life."

Fred Fuld III

Chapter 26

Interesting Investment Quotations

"The most important thing to do if you find yourself in a hole is to stop digging." Warren Buffett, billionaire businessman

"Before you invest, investigate." William Arthur Ward, author and educator

"If I try my best and fail, well, I've tried my best." Steve Jobs, founder of Apple

"The man who has done his level best…is a success, even though the world writes him down a failure." B.C. Forbes

"Coming together is a beginning, staying together is progress, and working together is success. " Henry Ford, automobile businessman

"With an evening coat and a white tie, anybody, even a stock broker, can gain a reputation for being civilized." Oscar Wilde, poet and playwright

"Money. The ultimate motivation. The ultimate way of keeping score." Michael Connelly, author

"Never invest in anything that eats or needs repainting." Billy Rose, composer and entrepreneur

"To be successful, you must decide exactly what you want to accomplish, then resolve to pay the price to get it." Bunker Hunt, oil businessman

"Emotions are your worst enemy in the stock market." Don Hays, stock market commentator

"The lesson of Buffett was: To succeed in a spectacular fashion you had to be spectacularly unusual." Michael Lewis, author of *The Big Short*

"I never attempt to make money on the stock market. I buy on the assumption that they could close the market the next day and not reopen it for five years." Warren Buffett, businessman and investor

"That some achieve great success, is proof to all that others can achieve it as well." Abraham Lincoln, former president of the United States

"Everyone has the brainpower to follow the stock market. If you made it through fifth-grade math, you can do it." Peter Lynch, money manager

"The collective insecurity of the world makes it easy for people to hit home runs while everyone is aiming for base hits." — Timothy Ferriss, author

"Gentlemen prefer bonds." Andrew Mellon, businessman and financier

"The stock market has forecast nine of the last five recessions" Paul A. Samuelson, economist

"The arts are an even better barometer of what is happening in our world than the stock market or the debates in congress." Hendrik Willem Van Loon, historian and journalist

"If stock market experts were so expert, they would be buying stock, not selling advice." Norman R. Augustine, aerospace businessman

"Now is always the most difficult time to invest." Anonymous

"I can't figure the stock market out. I think it's wacky. I have done well with a long-term strategy and will continue being a long-term investor." Scott McNealy, businessman, co-founded Sun Microsystems

"One of the funny things about the stock market is that every time one person buys, another sells, and both think they are astute." William Feather, publisher and author

"It's easy to grin when your ships come in and you've got the stock market beat, but the man worth while is the man who can smile when his pants are too tight in the seat" Anonymous

"The most valuable things in life are not measured in monetary terms. The really important things are not houses and lands, stocks and bonds, automobiles and real state, but friendships, trust, confidence, empathy, mercy, love and faith." Bertrand Russell, philosopher

"Stock prices have reached what looks like a permanently high plateau." Irving Fisher, economist

"A stockbroker urged me to buy a stock that would triple its value every year. I told him, 'At my age, I don't even buy green bananas.'" Claude Pepper, politician

"If you hear that everybody is buying a certain stock, ask who is selling." James Dines, investment newsletter writer

"I made my money by selling too soon." Bernard Baruch, financier and economist

"If a little money does not go out, great money will not come in." Confucius, philosopher

"An investment in knowledge always pays the best interest. " Benjamin Franklin, author, printer, inventor, diplomat, scientist

"Money & success don't change people; they merely amplify what is already there." Will Smith

"Don't gamble; take all your savings and buy some good stock and hold it till it goes up, then sell it. If it don't go up, don't buy it." Will Rogers, cowboy, entertainer, humorist

When asked what the stock market will do, J.P Morgan (banker, financier, businessman) replied: "It will fluctuate."

"Bulls make money. Bears make money. Pigs get slaughtered." Anonymous

"Don't try to buy at the bottom and sell at the top. It can't be done except by liars." Bernard Baruch, financier and economist

"If your stocks worry you, sell to the sleeping point." Joseph D. Goodman, the first Forbes columnist

"The fishing is best where the fewest go." Timothy Ferriss, author

"Be bullish in a bull market, but don't be either a bull or a bear all the time." Joseph D. Goodman, the first Forbes columnist

"Never allow the fear of striking out keep you from playing the game!" Babe Ruth

"Success is doing what you want to do, when you want, where you want, with whom you want, as much as you want." Anthony Robbins

Chapter 27

Stock Market Trivia Quiz

Let's see if you know this trivia. Some was previously covered in this book, some wasn't. The answers are shown at the end.

1. What was the original business of Berkshire Hathaway when Warren Buffett first started buying shares?
a. textiles
b. investing
c. insurance
d. coal
e. food
f. oil & gas

2. Which of the following jobs did Warren Buffet have when he was young?
a. newspaper delivery boy
b. running a pinball machine business
c. stealing golf balls
d. all of the above

3. What is the oldest stock exchange in the United States?
a. Philadelphia Stock Exchange
b. New York Stock Exchange
c. Boston Stock Exchange
d. Pacific Coast Stock Exchange

4. What is the oldest commodities exchange in the U.S.?

a. Chicago Board of Trade

b. Kansas City Board of Trade

c. New York Cotton Exchange

d. New York Mercantile Exchange

5. The highest priced share of stock that ever traded was of what company?

a. Yahoo! Japan

b. Berkshire Hathaway

c. Indians Inc.

d. Mechanics Bank

e. Google

6. Who said, "An investment in knowledge always pays the best interest"?

a. Benjamin Franklin

b. Bernard Baruch

c. J.P Morgan

d. Warren Buffett

7. The country with the highest inflation rate in 2008 was

a. Zimbabwe

b. Ethiopia

c. Venezuela

d. Mongolia

8. On the day after every presidential election since 1896, what percentage of the time was the Dow Jones Industrial Average up for the day?

a. 48%

b. 76%

c. 23%

d. 81%

9. Which of the following companies are owned by Berkshire Hathaway?
a. Dairy Queen
b. World Book Encyclopedias
c. See's Candies
d. GEICO
e. all of the above

10. What is the symbol for American Telephone & Telegraph?
a. A
b. AT
c. ATT
d. T

Answers:

1.a., 2.d., 3.a., 4.a., 5.a., 6.a., 7.a., 8.a., 8.d, 10.a.

SPECIAL SECTION:
THE WEIRD WORDS OF WALL STREET

Making Sense of Stock and Bond Gibberish

Air Pocket Stock

This kind of stock can give your portfolio a bumpy ride and can empty your pocket. There are actually two definitions of an air pocket stock.

The first definition is a stock that quickly plummets for no company-related reason whatsoever, just like a jet running into an air pocket. The reason for the drop can be due to several reasons, including a large investor unloading shares, an institution dumping shares, or just a temporary imbalance of buy and sell orders.

The second definition is very similar; it is a stock that plunges due to news that crops up unexpectedly. For example, the sudden death or resignation of a high level company officer, the recall of a product or drug due to a major problem, or an announcement of an investigation by the Securities and Exchange Commission regarding financial shenanigans.

Alligator Spread

Think of the alligator as your brokerage firm eating away at your profits. An alligator spread is an options spread where the investor can't make money due to the commissions involved.

An option spread is when you buy and short options at the same time on the same stock at either different strike prices, and/or different expirations, or it could involve buying both a call and put option on the same stock or shorting both calls and puts at the same time.

Sometimes spreads have to move a huge amount just to break even, especially with very low priced options. An alligator spread can take place when an investor legs into a spread, in other words, places an order for each part of the spread at separate times.

Angel

An angel, also known as an angel investor or a business angel, is an individual who invests in a business start-up and is given an interest in the company in return for the investment. Angels are usually wealthy individuals who invest their own funds. Angels have been the primary funders of Broadway plays for many years.

Once a business owner has tapped friends and family members, the next alternative is the angel. Because of the very high risk of the investment, angels generally expect a very high return on investment. This is due to the fact that angels realize that some of their investments will become worthless, so they need extremely high returns to offset those losses.

Baby Bond

Baby bonds are bonds that are issued in very small denominations. Currently bonds are issued in $5,000 denominations. However, many years ago, and as late as the 1970's, investors could occasionally find bonds in $1,000 denominations, which were often referred to as "baby bonds".

There are other bonds with extremely small denominations, usually in the amount of $25 or $100, which trade on the major exchanges, similar to stocks. However, they are often referred to as mini-bonds or micro-bonds.

The original baby bonds were issued by the state of Louisiana during the 1800's (see the above picture). The reasons these bonds were called baby bonds were threefold: they had extremely small denominations of $5 each, the size of the certificates were a very small (less than the width of a dollar bill measuring approximately 3" by 4.25"), and last but not least, they had a vignette of a baby on them.

Backwardation

Backwardation, also referred to as normal backwardation, takes place when the price of a futures contract, such a for oil or natural gas, is trading below the expected spot price at maturity.

The term comes from the word "backward" and came into use in the mid-1800's, when sellers of stock would pay a fee to delay the delivery of the stock.

The opposite of backwardation is called Contango.

Barbell

The barbell is an investment strategy that involves buying two opposite but related type of securities.

There are a couple types of barbell strategies, sometimes referred to as dumbbell strategies. The stock barbell strategy, recommended by a few top investment advisors, which involves investing half the portfolio in high yield stocks to provide income and stability, and the other half in low priced undervalued speculative stocks.

The other type of barbell strategy relates to bonds. It involves the purchase of long-term bonds, usually with maturities of 30 years, in order to provide the portfolio with high income, and the purchase of very short-term bonds or notes, which would provide liquidity to the portfolio.

The reason why these strategies are referred to as barbells is because they involve the purchase of investments at both ends of the spectrum, like a barbell having weights on each end, while avoiding anything in the middle.

BATS

You may think that BATS are mammals that fly around the air, but BATS is the third largest stock market in the United States. BATS actually has two exchanges, the BZX Exchange and the BYX Exchange.

The holding company for BATS was founded in July 2005 in the Kansas City, Missouri area. BATS stands for Better Alternative Trading System. Trading on BATS amounts to over 10% of all U.S. equity trading on a daily basis.

Bear

A bear is someone who believes the stock market will go down. A bear market is a falling market. Where does the term bear come from? Some sources say that since a bear knocks you down, it is like a falling market. However, the term came about during the 18th century relating to the bearskin market.

See Chapter 1 for more details.

The book, Every Man His Own Broker, published in 1775, contains the first usage of the words Bull and Bear as types of investors. It was written by Thomas Mortimer. Pages have been reprinted enlarged on the following pages for easier reading.

EVERY MAN
HIS OWN
BROKER:
OR,
A GUIDE to EXCHANGE-ALLEY.

IN WHICH

The Nature of the several FUNDS, vulgarly called the STOCKS, is clearly explained, and accurate Computations are formed of the Average Value of EAST-INDIA STOCKS for several Years, from the current Year.

The Mystery and Iniquity of STOCK-JOBBING is laid before the Public in a New and Impartial Light.

The Method of Transferring STOCK, and of Buying and Selling the several GOVERNMENT SECURITIES, without the Assistance of a BROKER, is made intelligible to the meanest Capacity: and an Account is given of the Laws in force relative to BROKERS, Clerks at the Bank, &c. With Directions how to avoid the Losses that are frequently sustained by the Destruction of BANK NOTES, INDIA BONDS, &c. by Fires and other Accidents.

WITH

An Historical Account of the Origin, Progress, and present State of PUBLIC-CREDIT, BANKING, and the SINKING-FUND.

To which is now added

A SUPPLEMENT, containing RULES for forming a Judgment of the real Causes of the Rise or Fall of the STOCKS; and several useful TABLES of INTEREST, &c.

rigid facidunt leges, ubi sola pecunia regnat.

The EIGHTH EDITION, Altered and Enlarged.

By THOMAS MORTIMER, Esq.
Author of the ELEMENTS of Commerce, Politics, and Finance.

LONDON,
Printed for S. HOOPER, No. 25, Ludgate-hill. MDCCLXXV.

his long and faithful fervices in parliament, fome regulations propofed by him, were paffed into a law, in the year 1734, under the title of "*An act for the better preventing the infamous practice of Stock-jobbing;*" by which the moft palpable and glaring frauds then in vogue, were indeed fuppreffed : the BUBBLES burft, and the RACE HORSES of Exchange-Alley, expired with the date of that act; but BULLS and BEARS ftill exift in full vigour. The rejected part of Sir John Barnard's fcheme for the total extirpation of Stock-jobbers, was brought into parliament laft feffions with fome alterations, and was again thrown out by the houfe of lords; and fuch muft be the fate of all fchemes of the fame nature, in which public regifters are propofed to be kept, of thofe

6.

Bear Raid

A bear raid is a technique used by short sellers to drive down the price of a stock. This can be done several ways.

It can be done by cranking up the rumor mill with real or imagined bad news and innuendos. Dumping of existing large holdings of the stock can also cause the price to tank. And finally, naked short selling (described later) can also make the stock plummet. Naked short selling is illegal, and is difficult to do these days.

Bear trap

A bear trap is a situation where an investor sees that a stock or the stock market in general is dropping and expects a continued drop, so the investor sells shares currently owned or shorts shares, expecting to make money from the decline.

Unfortunately, it is just a temporary downturn, and the investment moves up, creating a 'trap' and either loss of money if shorting or loss of opportunity cost if selling a stock that is owned.

Boiler Room

Definition 1:

A boiler room is a company where salesmen sit around in close quarters making phone calls all day long, trying to sell investments (usually worthless penny stocks) to unsuspecting investors.

Definition 2:

Boiler Room was the name of a movie made in 2000 about a young college dropout who becomes a stockbroker for a brokerage firm that specializes in promoting low-priced but intrinsically worthless stocks.

Blank Check

A blank check isn't something you send to a boiler room stockbroker. Basically, Blank Check is a type of company that raises money but doesn't tell you what it's going to use the money for.

A blank check company is a generally a development stage company that doesn't have a specific business plan or if it does have a plan, has indicated its plan is to engage in a merger or acquisition of another company. These companies are typically very speculative investments, and have additional restrictions from the Securities and Exchange Commission.

Blind Pool

The term Blind Pool Company has been used interchangeably with Blank Check Company. It is basically a company that raises money without any specific plans for the funds.

This term is usually applied towards a company raising money either through stock offering or limited partnership, where the investors don't know what assets or business will be purchased. Obviously very speculative.

Blue Sky Laws

Blue sky laws are state security laws with regulate how stocks are sold to the public. Generally, companies have to qualify under the blue sky laws of each state that the Initial Public Offering takes place.

The term comes from the statement made by Kansas Banking Commissioner J. N. Dolley in the early 1900's, "speculative schemes which have no more basis than so many feet of 'blue sky."

Burn Rate

No, burn rate is not the number of times you lost money in a bad stock. Burn rate, in very simple terms, is how long a company can stay in business losing money year after year, based on the amount of money the company has on hand.

The burn rate is usually examined for start-up biotechnology companies with no earnings. They spend huge amount of money on research, usually to come up with treatments and cures for cancer and other diseases.

Bust

Definition 1:

Broke, out of business, bankrupt, as in "the company went bust."

Definition 2:

To cancel a trade. If a trade is made in error, the trade is sometimes busted. This is very uncommon now as most trades are made electronically.

Butterfly

A butterfly is a type of stock option spread. To make it simply complicated, you short two calls on a stock, and buy one call with a higher strike price and buy one call with a lower strike price, all with the same expiration date.

Cash Cow

Better than a goose that lays one golden egg, a cash cow is a stock that generates a significant amount of cash flow and is expected to for many years.

The term is also used to refer to a business or division within a corporation that generates a disproportionately large amount of revenues to the company, far more than any of the other divisions.

Chinese Wall

A Chinese Wall is the division between various departments at investment bankers and stock brokerage firms.

For example, the research department of an investment company does not interact with the department that handles initial public offerings, so that there is no conflict of interest.

Churn

Churning is the inappropriate buying and selling of stocks by a stockbroker of a client's account for no purpose other than to generate commissions for themselves.

This is illegal, of course, and not as common as it used to be, when there were no online brokerage firms, and investors were forced to deal with individual stockbrokers.

Collar

A collar is an investment strategy used to protect a huge gain in a stock. It is usually done by buying puts on the stock, but can also be done by shorting the stock.

Collars are often used by investors that want to roll their capital gain into the following year, while avoiding the risk of th stock dropping while waiting until the end of the year. They are also used by investors that owned restricted stock that they are unable to sell for a period of time, and they are concerned about the stock dropping before the lock-up period ends.

Contango

Contango is the opposite of Backwardation. Contango is when the future price of a commodity is more than the current price, also known as the spot price.

The word is reportedly a derivation of the words continuation, continue, and contingent, and came in to usage in Great Britain in the 1800's.

Coupon Clipper

Definition 1:

In the old days, bearer bonds were issued with sheets of coupons attached. Each coupon represented one period's interest payment, usually the interest for six months. The investor, the "coupon clipper," would cut off the latest coupon with scissors, and take the coupon to the bank to either cash it or deposit the funds.

Definition 2:

A very wealthy, yet thrifty, person who clips coupons out of the newspaper in order to save money.

Dead Cat Bounce

A dead cat bounce takes place when a stock rises slightly after dropping hard and fast. When bad stocks ("dead cats") drop quickly, there is usually a slight bounce, due to either bargain hunters buying and/or short sellers covering their position.

This term first appeared in The Financial Times in 1985. The idea behind the term is that anything bounces if it has a large drop, even a dead cat.

Dead Peasant Policy

A Dead Peasant Policy is a corporate owned life insurance policy, which insures the lives on a company's employees with, in one form, the beneficiary being the corporation. These policies have often been written without the employee's knowledge or consent.

So for example, if a factory worker were to die, the company could collect the insurance proceeds on that employee.

There are tax benefits to the corporations with these insurance policies. Recently, the government has created restrictions on the use of these policies, so they are not as common as they used to be.

Dogs of the Dow

The Dogs of the Dow are the ten stocks in the Dow Jones Industrial Average with the highest yields.

This also refers to the investment technique of buying the ten highest yielding stocks of the Dow, and each year, adjusting the portfolio to maintain the ten highest yielders.

DRIP

DRIP stands for Dividend Reinvestment Plan. This is an investment plan where the dividends are automatically reinvested in the stock.

Many investors like these plans because of the convenience, the automation, and avoidance of paying commissions on these small investments.

Elephant

An elephant is a very large institutional investor, such as a mutual fund, hedge fund, or pension plan.

They are referred to a elephants because they are so large and can move markets when they make investments.

Fallen Angel

A stock or bond that was considered high quality but has fallen out of favor and fallen in price.

A historical example is Penn Central, which was once a high quality stock back when railroads were popular, that eventually fell out of favor.

Falling Knife

This is something that you should never try to catch. A falling knife is a stock that has had a significant drop, which may trick investors to think they are getting a bargain because the price is so low.

The problem is that the falling knife will continue to drop and cut the hand (figuratively speaking, of course) of the investors who end up buying it, causing the investors to get burned, or hurt following the same analogy.

Fannie Mae

Fannie Mae is the nickname for the acronym FNMA, which stands for Federal National Mortgage Association.

FNMA is a publicly traded company, founded in 1938, securitizes mortgage loans on single family and multi-family residential properties.

Fill or Kill (FOK)

Fill or Kill is a type of stock order where an immediate limit order is placed on a large number of shares, and if the order isn't filled right away for all the shares, it is cancelled instantly.

Fill means place the order. Kill means cancel the order. The acronym for this type of order is FOK. It could be for a buy order or a sell order.

Flipper

Definition 1:

A real estate investor who buys a house, quickly fixes it up, and immediately resells it for a profit.

Definition 2:

A stock market investor who buys hot stock issues on an IPO and sells the stock right away for a huge profit.

Definition 3:

This term is sometimes used to refer to a day trader who buys and sells stocks on the same day, flipping the stocks.

Float

It's not something that comes with root beer. Float, also known as public float or free float, refers to the number of shares of a corporation that can be actively traded. This number of shares is less than the total outstanding shares.

The float is the number of outstanding shares less the number of closely held or restricted shares. These are usually shares that are owned by top executives of the company.

Freddie Mac

Freddie Mac is the nickname for the acronym FHLMC, which stands for Federal Home Loan Mortgage Association.

Freddie Mac was founded in 1970 to provide a secondary market for mortgages, buy buying them, packaging them together, and reselling the mortgage pools to institutions and investors.

Goob

A goob, and occasionally referred to as a goober, is a commission point (commission dollar) on a stock or a commission percent on a bond. For example, if a stock IPO price is $50 and one dollar is paid to the brokerage firm as a commission, then the stock has a commission of one goob.

If a municipal bond sale paid the broker two percent, then the bond would have two goobs as a commission.

This term became popular with the Southern California stock brokerage firms during the late 1970's and early 1980's, probably not coincidentally during the time that Jimmy Carter, a former peanut farmer, was president.

Green Shoe

If you think a green shoe is an expensive pair of loafers that you paid for with money you made in the stock market, sorry, you would be wrong. If you think it is a shoe that is made out of environmentally conscious materials, you would still be wrong.

A green shoe, also referred to as a greenshoe, refers to the overallotment of shares or limited partnership interests for issues where the demand for the investment is much larger than anticipated.

Greater Fools

Great fools are the investors you sell a stock to after it has gone up a huge amount.

The Greater Fool Theory is that you can buy a stock at an outrageously over-priced amount in a hot market because (you think) you can resell it to a greater fool at a higher price.

Iron Butterfly

For investors, an Iron Butterfly is not a psychedelic rock bank.

An iron butterfly is an option trading technique where the trader shorts an at-the-money strike price strangle and buys an out of the money strangle at the same time on the same stock.

Iron Condor

This is an option technique that combines a vertical put spread and a vertical call spread, all with different strike prices but the same expiration date on the same stock.

Junk bond

A junk bond is a low quality bond, usually with a rating below BBB or Baa. These are considered to be "below bank quality" bonds.

Junk bonds generally pay yields that are much higher than other bonds in order to compensate investors for the higher risk of default.

These bonds are also sometimes referred to as speculative grade bonds and non-investment grade bonds.

Kill

No, this is not something you do to your stockbroker after he sells you shares of Enron at the top of the market.

Kill means to cancel a stock trade or order. If an investor places a limit order, and decides to cancel it before it is transacted, it is considered killing the order.

Lame Duck

The book, *Every Man His Own Broker*, published in 1775, describes lame ducks as "those who refuse to fulfill their contracts." This related to what short sellers did (and still do). A short seller is someone who does a stock transaction in the hopes that a stock will drop in price. A short sale is when an investor sells a stock that he doesn't have (he technically borrows the stock from the brokerage firm to sell) then buys it back at a later time at, hopefully, a lower price (when he technically takes the stock that he bought and returns it to the brokerage firm). The difference between the sale price and purchase price is his profit (or loss if he has to buy it back at a higher price).

In modern day terminology, lame duck means a short seller than can't cover his position.

LEAPS

The term LEAPS refers to Long Term Equity Anticipation Securities. These are basically long term call options on stocks and ETFs.

LEAPS are generally issued for two to five year time frames.

Leg

Noun: One part of an option strategy. In other words, if you buy a call and a put on the same stock, each option is considered a leg.

Verb: To transact one part of an investment strategy, one leg at a time, as opposed to investing in the entire strategy all at once. For example, "I legged into the option positions because I thought I could get better prices."

Lipstick Index

Leonard Lauder, the chairman of the board of Estee Lauder, came up with the Lipstick Index, which reportedly showed that lipstick purchases increased during economic downturns, since women would be more likely spend money on smaller purchases such as lipstick, as opposed to purchasing clothing.

This index was later shown to not be true, as lipstick purchases increased during economic boons, and dropped during recessions.

Naked Shorts

Naked shorts exist when a short seller shorts a stock but hasn't borrowed the stock to sell to create the short position.

Previously, short sellers could "gang up" on a stock by selling the shares without having the shares to sell, thereby driving down the price of the stock, just from the huge volume of selling. Currently, with trades being electronic, it should theoretically be impossible to do short selling without having the stock to sell, at least by individual investors, but there are claims that the practice is still being done by companies, through some exemptions.

Poison Pill

A poison pill is a provision in a company's corporate charter to prevent an unwanted takeover by another company. This is also known as a shareholder rights plan.

The poison pill is triggered when an investor accumulates a certain percentage of the outstanding shares, giving the other shareholders the right to buy the stock at a discount.

Rounded Bottom

A rounded bottom is a term used by technical analysts to refer to the fact that a stock's chart shows a gradual drop, a bottoming out, then a gradual rise; in other words , a curved "U" shape.

This would be as opposed to a "V" shape which would be a sharp drop in price with an immediate sharp rise.

Seat

A seat in stock market terms, is not a place where you sit. A seat is a membership of a stock exchange. Previously, these seats, or memberships, could be bought and sold just like a stock. They could even be rented or leased out.

These seats were owned by stock brokerage firms, floor traders, and market makers, which allowed them to trade on the exchange. Exchanges such as the New York Stock Exchange, the American Stock Exchange, and the Pacific Stock Exchange had active trading markets in their seats.

The term originally came from the fact that the early exchanges gave traders assigned chairs to sit in.

Sin Stocks

A sin stock is a stock of a company that many people consider inappropriate for their investment dollar, from a moral or ethical standpoint. Sometimes these are referred to as socially irresponsible stocks.

These include companies in such businesses as gambling and casinos, alcohol, adult entertainment, and tobacco. Some investors even consider firearms companies and defense contractors as sin stocks.

Certain organizations and individuals include condom and birth control companies as sinful stocks, and some even consider private prison companies as sin stocks.

Skirt Length Indicator

The skirt length indicator is supposedly a sign of how the stock market is performing or will perform based on the length of women's skirts.

During the Roaring 20's, hemlines rose from ankle length to knee length with the era of the flappers. Concurrently, the stock market was roaring upwards. Skirt lengths started to drop around 1928 and 1929, and the market crashed in October of 1929.

During the 1960's, the era of the miniskirt, skirt length rose from calf length to way above the knees and the stock market rose along with the hemlines.

In the early 1970's, the midi-skirt and ankle length skirts came back into fashion, and the stock market experienced the 1973-1974 crash.

Now the skirt length, along with the stock market, is all over the place.

Splits

A split is when a corporation increases the number of shares, giving shareholders a greater number of shares, yet having no intrinsic change to the shareholder's investment.

In other words, if a stock is trading at $80 a share, and the shareholder has 100 shares, after a stock split, the shareholder would have 200 shares trading at $40 a share, assuming no other external factors affect the share price.

Two for one stock splits are most common, but a stock can split one-and-a-half for one, three for one, ten for one or any other combination. There can even be a reverse split, such as a one for five.

Spreads

There are numerous definitions of "spread" in the finance industry. Here are just a few of them.

1. The difference between the bid and asked price on a stock. So if a stock is bid at 10.25 and the asked price is 10.45, the spread is twenty cents.

2. An option trading strategy where two or more options are bought and/or sold on the same stock.

3. The difference between the rates of return on two different investments. For example, the difference between junk bonds and AAA bonds.

Strangle

Strangle- What you do to your stockbroker after he sells you dot com stocks at the top of the market. Not really, just kidding.

A strangle is an options technique using an out of the money call and an out of the money put. The strangle can either be bought or sold (shorted).

The name strangle comes from the fact that if you short the strangle, and the stock makes a huge move, either up or down, especially up since your loss could be unlimited, you can get financially strangled and wiped out.

STRIPS

STRIPS is the abbreviation for Separate Trading of Registered Interest and Principal Securities.

Coupons are removed (stripped) from regular coupon bonds by investment brokers to create zero coupon bonds, known as STRIPS.

Ticker

Definition 1:

A ticker, also called stock ticker, refers to the stock symbol made up with a series of letters that is used to place orders to buy a stock.

Definition 2:

A stock ticker was the equipment under a glass dome that printed out the prices of stocks on strips of paper. See the picture above.

Tombstone

A tombstone is a very plain text-only ad that appears in financial publications, such as the Wall Street Journal, to announce initial public offerings (IPOs) and secondary offerings. Sometimes these are published in advance of the offerings and sometimes after the offering.

It basically has the name of the company, the number or shares offered and/or the dollar amount, and the underwriters.

A tombstone ad from 1920

Torpedo Stock

A perfect example of a torpedo stock is Enron, after it reached its peak, started to drop, and the bad news started coming out. The stock tanked, and just kept tanking.

So a torpedo stock is a stock that is dropping, dropping fast, and will never recover. This could be due to terrible news about the company or fraud, or both.

Walking Dead

This term started coming in to use back in the 1980's when venture capital limited partnerships first became popular. After several years into the partnership, the companies in the portfolios would be described four different ways: ten-baggers, doubles, walking-deads, and busts.

The walking-deads were the companies that will continue to stumble along forever, never becoming extremely successful but never going out of business. And probably never taken over by another company. Therefore, walking dead.

These days, the walking dead are stocks of companies that won't go bankrupt but will never really go up in value.

Whale

A whale is an investor with a lot of money available for investing, usually a fairly wealthy individual.

Usually the stockbrokers in the boiler rooms would talk about "bagging a whale" or "catching a whale." This means that they were able to get the investor to buy a pump and dump stock.

Sources

Much of the information in this book has been collected for many years, through my own personal knowledge and experience. Yahoo, Google, and Wikipedia along with numerous other websites were used to confirm data that was used. The following include some of the primary sources for some of the chapters.

Chapter 1

Every Man His Own Broker, by Thomas Mortimer

Chapter 3

National Stock Summary

http://www.naturalbridgeva.com/natural-bridge-history.php

Chapter 4

New York Stock Exchange, nyse.com

Chapter 5

Sales data from Domaining.com

Chapter 8

Pink Sheets

Yahoo! Finance

Chapter 9

Goetzmann, William N. *Financing Civilization.*
http://viking.som.yale.edu/will/finciv/chapter1.htm

Goetzmann, William N., Rouwenhorst, K. Geert, editors. *The Origins of Value: The Financial Innovations that Created Modern Capital Markets*

Van De Mieroop, Marc. *Society and Enterprise in Old Babylonian Ur.*

Chapter 10

Footnoted.org

Bank Note Reporter

New York Stock Exchange, nyse.com

Chapter 11

www.douala-stock-exchange.com

Chapter 12

Marinol.com

Solvay.com

Chapter 13

Finance.yahoo.com

Thehotpennystocks.com

Chapter 14

Imdb.com

Chapter 15

U. S. Patent & Trademark Office

Chapter 17

Walker, Stephen Todd *Wave Theory For Alternative Investments: Riding The Wave with Hedge Funds, Commodities, and Venture Capital*

Chapter 19

New York Stock Exchange, nyse.com

Chapter 21

Antiquestocks.com

Coxrail.com, Terry Cox

Chapter 22

Gabriel, Mary. *Notorious Victoria*

Goldsmith, Barbara. *Other Powers*

Beachy Underhill, Lois. *The Woman Who Ran for President*

Sachs, Emanie. *The Terrible Siren*

Chapter 23

MacKay, Charles. *Extraordinary Popular Delusions and the Madness of Crowds*

Picture Credits

Most of the pictures were taken or scanned by the author.

Chapter 1

From the author's own collection.

Chapter 2

From the author's own collection.

Chapter 8

From the author's own collection.

Chapter 9

From the author's own collection.

Chapter 20

From the author's own collection.

Chapter 22

Library of Congress

Baby Bond

From the author's own collection.

Bear

From the author's own collection.

ABOUT THE AUTHOR

Fred Fuld III, is a financial historian. He was a former executive in the financial services industry who started out working as a stockbroker, and later as a market maker on the options floor of the Pacific Stock Exchange. He also worked as an adjunct professor for the College of Business of a California State University.

He started collecting antique stock certificates and other financial service industry collectibles many years ago. He then began selling antique stock certificates through his firm, Investment Research Institute, and later, antiquestocks.com.

He is the publisher of Stockerblog.com and the founder of WallStreetNewsNetwork.com, and has written numerous articles for various publications, including Friends of Financial History Magazine, the Bond and Share Society Journal, and Scripophily Magazine. He has been interviewed on CNBC, Fox Business News, and Globo TV.

Made in the USA
Charleston, SC
04 November 2013